Are you a Dragonfly?

For Kit-J.A.

For the Ladies of Holsworthy Library-T.H.

SRAonline.com

SRA

Copyright © 2008 by SRA/McGraw-Hill.

Printed in the U.S.A.

Send all inquiries to:
SRA/McGraw-Hill
4400 Easton Commons
Columbus, OH 43219-6188

ISBN 978-0-07-612266-0
MHID 0-07-612266-2

10 LHN 22

The McGraw-Hill Companies

Are you a Dragonfly?

Judy Allen and Tudor Humphries

McGraw Hill SRA

Columbus, OH

Are you a dragonfly?

If you are, your mother laid her eggs in the stems of a water plant.

You swam out of one of them–and so did lots of others just like you.

You are VERY small.

You are very hungry.

And guess what?
You can breathe water through
the end of your tail.

Eat and grow.

Eat tiny water creatures.

You have a special grabber for catching them. It's called a mask because it covers half your face.

Creep up on your prey—
then shoot out your mask
and grab it.

Eat and grow
until your skin
is so tight you
have to take it off.

Then eat and grow
some more, and do it again.

And again.

And again.

Don't worry, there will always be new skin underneath.

Now that you
have grown larger,
you can eat larger food.
Try a tadpole or a small fish.

But be careful-there are plenty
who would like to eat YOU.
Beware of water beetles.
Water beetles
pounce!

Beware of ducks.
Ducks dive,
and they're
BIG.

Two years have passed. You're bored with life in the water.

Crawl up a plant stem into the air.

Do this at night so birds don't see you and eat you.

Hold on tight. As you dry your skin splits one more time.

Slowly, slowly,
climb out
of your
old skin.

First pull
your head free.
Then pull
your legs free.

Flop over backward
and have a rest.

Now lean
forward, grab
your old skin,
and pull your
whole body out.

Guess what? Now
you can breathe air
through tiny holes on
the sides of your body.

You're a dragonfly!

At first you're very pale and crumpled.

But your beautiful colors will come, and your two pairs of wings will straighten out.

You're a fantastic flyer.

You can fly fast,

you can hover,

you can even
fly backward.

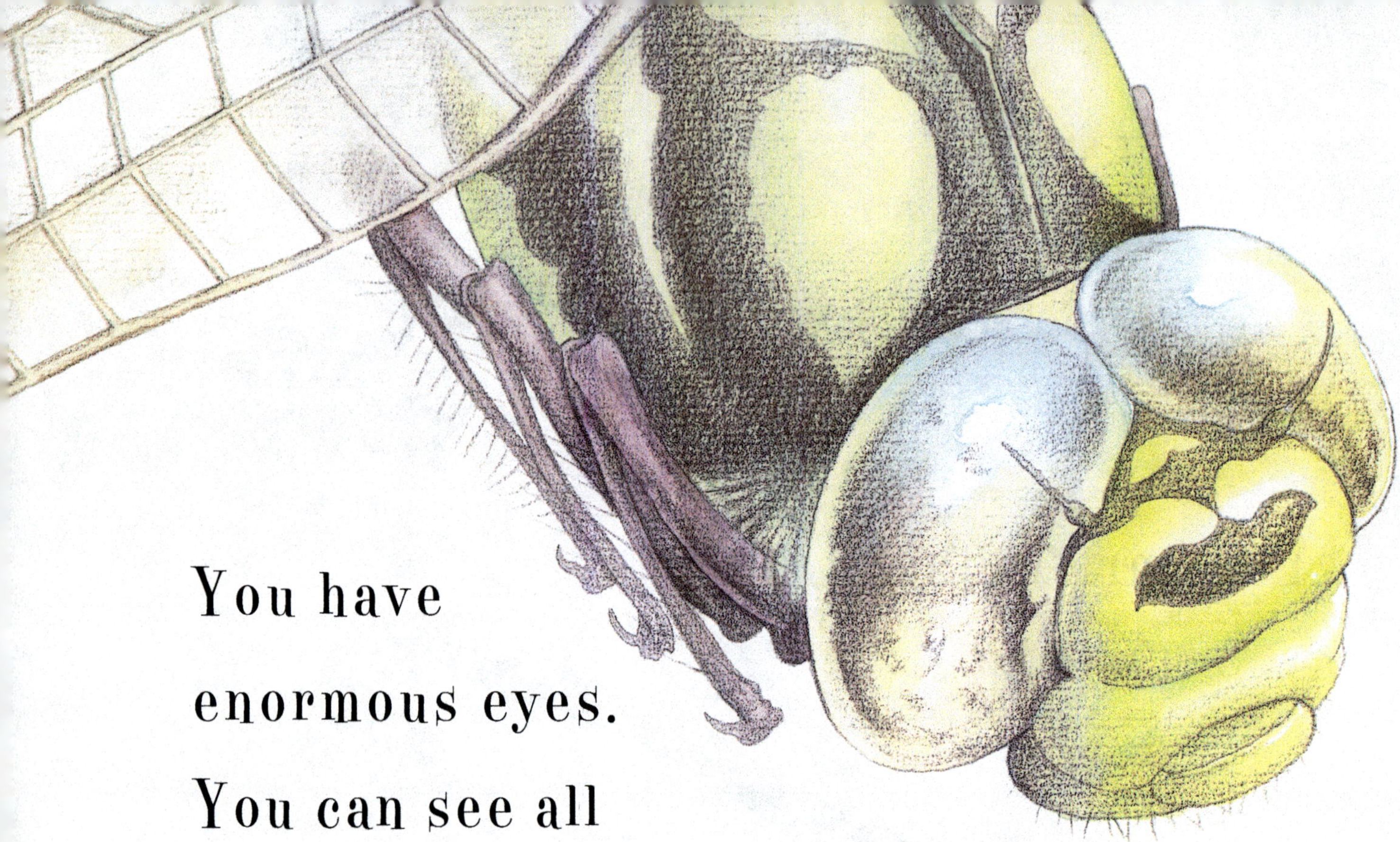

You have
enormous eyes.
You can see all
around you, all the time.

You can see what's behind you,
in front of you, above you,
below you, and beside you.

This is very useful
when you're looking for food.

This is also very useful when
you are dodging hungry birds
and avoiding spider's webs.

You were a fierce hunter
underwater-now you are
a fierce hunter in the air.

Hunt over ponds and streams
and slow-flowing rivers.
Hunt over marshes
and in forests.

Hold your legs out in front of you to catch your prey.

Hunt midges and mosquitoes, flies, wasps, and small butterflies.

When you catch something, eat it.

You are a hawker-
you hunt while you're flying.

This dragonfly is a darter-
it sits still until it sees its prey,
then it darts out and grabs it.

This is not a dragonfly at all.
It's a damselfly. It's thinner and
lighter and slower than you.
It likes to pick small insects
off leaves and flowers.

Now look around you.

If you and all your friends look a little

like this

or this

or this

you are not a
dragonfly.
You are...

...a human child.

You can't fly.

You can't breathe underwater.

It's very unlikely that you have
a mask attached to your face.

But you can do a lot of things
that dragonflies can't do.

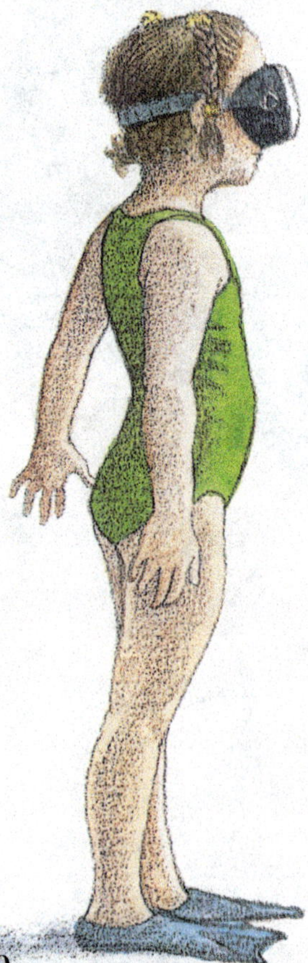

You don't have to keep
taking your skin off,
and you don't have to eat
midges and mosquitoes.

Best of all, you'll never, ever **EVER** be eaten by a duck.

Did You Know...

... there are more than 4,800 different kinds of dragonflies.

...dragonflies are among the oldest winged insects. They've been on the earth for about 300 million years–long before the dinosaurs.

...dragonflies have two pairs of wings. They can beat each pair separately, which is why they are such great flyers.

...dragonflies usually rest with their wings spread out, but damselflies usually fold their wings above their backs, the way butterflies do.